Contents

Words in **bold** are in the glossary on page 31.

Mountain Habitats

One-fifth of our planet is covered by mountains. One-tenth of all the people in the world live in mountain regions, and millions more rely on them for water, wood from the forests and substances found below Earth's surface.

Rocky ridges

Great mountain ranges can be found on most **continents**. The Andes is the longest, stretching 7,000 km down the western coast of South America. The Rocky Mountains in North America make up the second-longest range. The Himalayas, in Asia, contain the world's highest peaks, including Mount Everest. In Australia, the Great Dividing Range runs down the whole of the eastern coastline, and in Europe, the Alps stretch east to west across six countries.

▼ *This map shows some of the major mountain ranges, but mountains can be found all over the world.*

Yellow-legged frog (page 22)

Rocky Mountains

North America

Pacific Ocean

Andes

South America

Junin flightless grebe (page 26)

EXTREME ANIMALS

Chamois – a type of goat found in the European Alps – are among the fastest climbers in the world. They can clamber 600 m in just 10 minutes.

Mountain zones

Each mountain range is home to different plants and animals. Even within a mountain range, the **habitat** is divided into different regions, called zones, which have different characteristics. In the **foothills**, trees, grass and many other plants grow, and millions of animals make their homes. There may even be steamy tropical forests on the lower mountain slopes. Higher up, it gets colder and rockier. The trees thin out and eventually stop growing altogether. This is called the treeline. Beyond this, only the hardiest plants and animals can survive in the snowy landscape.

▲ *Mountain ranges, such as the Andes, are long chains of mountains that can stretch for thousands of kilometres.*

Asia

Europe
Alps

Middle East

Himalayas

Africa

Pacific Ocean

Australia

Great Dividing Range

Ethiopian wolf (page 15)

Giant panda (page 9)

Mountain gorilla (page 11)

Mountains Under Threat

The wood, water and other substances in mountain areas are valuable to people. Forests are cut down and the rock is blasted away in search of natural resources. Such activity causes great damage to the mountain environment and the creatures that live there.

Logging and mining

Mountain forests provide homes, shelter and food for many animal **species**, from tiny insects to huge gorillas. As large areas of forest are cut down, the animals either die or are forced to move into smaller areas. Competition for food becomes fierce, and some creatures cannot survive. Land is also cleared for mining, and the chemicals used in mining processes pollute the soil. The mountain habitat is left unusable for many years. Sometimes it never recovers.

◀ *This copper mine is in the Oquirrh Mountains in the western USA.*

WHAT DO YOU THINK?

Mountain regions are often rich in **minerals**, but mining disturbs mountain wildlife. What ways might there be of limiting the damage to the environment while accessing these precious **resources**?

ENDANGERED ANIMALS

The International Union for Conservation of Nature (IUCN, see page 28) lists animals according to how **endangered** they are.

Extinct: Died out completely.

Extinct in the wild: Only survive in captivity – for example, in zoos.

Critically endangered: Extremely high risk of becoming extinct in the near future.

Endangered: High risk of becoming extinct in the wild.

Vulnerable: High risk of becoming endangered in the wild.

Near threatened: Likely to become endangered in the near future.

Least concern: Lowest risk of becoming endangered.

Warming air and melting ice

Global warming is also affecting mountain habitats. As average temperatures rise around the world, animals that have **adapted** to living in cold mountain regions cannot cope with the changes to their environment. Some may move to higher **altitudes**, but not all creatures can move easily, or learn to live in a new habitat. Melting snow and **glaciers** are also changing the nature of mountain habitats. This affects the animals and people that live there.

▼ *Many glaciers are melting as global temperatures increase. This huge glacier is in Glacier Bay, Alaska.*

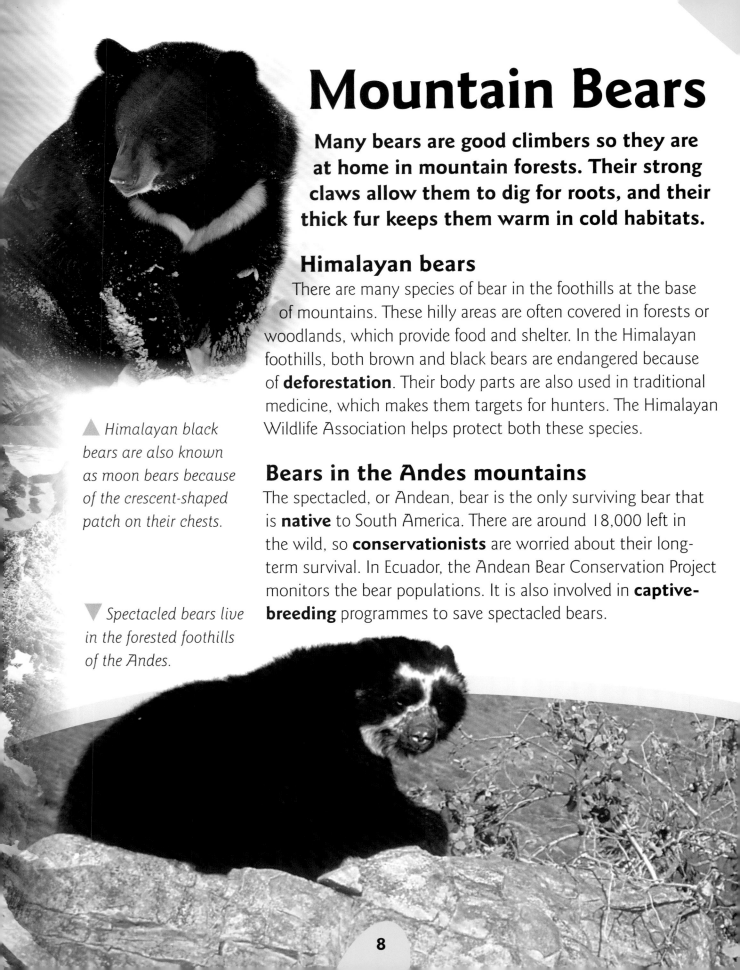

Mountain Bears

Many bears are good climbers so they are at home in mountain forests. Their strong claws allow them to dig for roots, and their thick fur keeps them warm in cold habitats.

Himalayan bears

There are many species of bear in the foothills at the base of mountains. These hilly areas are often covered in forests or woodlands, which provide food and shelter. In the Himalayan foothills, both brown and black bears are endangered because of **deforestation**. Their body parts are also used in traditional medicine, which makes them targets for hunters. The Himalayan Wildlife Association helps protect both these species.

▲ *Himalayan black bears are also known as moon bears because of the crescent-shaped patch on their chests.*

Bears in the Andes mountains

The spectacled, or Andean, bear is the only surviving bear that is **native** to South America. There are around 18,000 left in the wild, so **conservationists** are worried about their long-term survival. In Ecuador, the Andean Bear Conservation Project monitors the bear populations. It is also involved in **captive-breeding** programmes to save spectacled bears.

▼ *Spectacled bears live in the forested foothills of the Andes.*

SAVING WILDLIFE

Giant panda

About 1,600 giant pandas survive only in the bamboo forests of the high mountains in China. Habitat loss, **fragmentation** and **poaching** are just three of the threats that have made pandas the most famous endangered species in the world. WWF (see page 28) leads the way in panda **conservation**. It fights poaching, and has helped the Chinese government set up 50 nature **reserves** to protect the pandas.

▼ Many countries try to breed giant pandas in zoos, such as this one in China, but the bears do not thrive in captivity.

WHAT DO YOU THINK?

Some people think that too much money is spent on conserving giant pandas. They say it is too late to save them and efforts should be focused elsewhere. What are the arguments for and against saving wildlife that might be beyond long-term recovery?

1.5 m

Monkeys and Apes

Moving through the thick undergrowth and swinging between the trees of mountain forests, monkeys and apes are well adapted to this habitat. These animals live in several mountain zones, from the foothills to high up near the treeline.

Woolly monkeys

Yellow-tailed woolly monkeys inhabit the Andes mountains in Peru, South America. They live high in the trees, feeding on leaves, fruit and flowers. Until the 1950s, these monkeys lived so high up that they were not often affected by human activity, but then people began building houses, roads and farms in their forest habitat. Today there are fewer than 250 monkeys, and they are critically endangered. Yellow-tailed woolly monkeys have been named as a focal species by EDGE (see page 28) and now conservation programmes are underway.

◄ *Several types of South American monkey are listed by the IUCN, including Geoffroy's woolly monkey of Peru, which is endangered.*

Asian monkeys

Golden snub-nosed monkeys in the mountains of China have adapted to the very cold temperatures of their high habitat, where it often snows. Now, though, there are fewer than 15,000 left. Hunting for their golden fur was once the greatest threat, but today deforestation is a bigger danger. The Chinese government has made them a **protected species**, and a nature reserve has been set up to preserve their habitat.

▶ *The remaining snub-nosed monkeys live in mountain forests in China, at altitudes of up to 3,000 m.*

SAVING WILDLIFE

Mountain gorilla

Critically endangered mountain gorillas of central Africa are threatened by forest clearance, poaching, disease and **civil war**. In 1991 the International Gorilla Conservation Programme was set up to save the 880 mountain gorillas that are left. It works with professional African conservationists to educate local people and set up poaching patrols. It also encourages tourism to bring in money for further conservation.

▼ *A female mountain gorilla carries her baby in the Volcanoes National Park, Rwanda, central Africa.*

1.7 m

11

An Arabian leopard in captivity in the United Arab Emirates, in the Middle East. These big cats are being bred in zoos there.

Mountain Cats

Cats are sure-footed creatures and good climbers, so they are at home in mountain forests, especially in Asia, North and South America, and the Middle East.

Arabian leopards

The mountains of the Arabian Peninsula in the Middle East are home to a big cat on the edge of extinction. With only 200 Arabian leopards left, local groups formed the Arabian Leopard Trust in 1993, and began conserving the mountain habitat. The cats need large areas, because each adult has its own range and will attack others that come into its territory. Some of the leopards' range was made into a nature reserve, and later the leopards were protected by law from hunting. Arabian leopards have also been successfully bred in captivity.

Small cats of the Andes

Endangered Andean mountain cats are small wild **felines** — only around 60 cm long — that live high above the treeline in the Andes. There are around 2,500 of these little cats left in the wild. The roads and houses that have been built in their habitat have separated groups of the cats, which makes it difficult for them to find mates. Andean mountain cats are now a protected species. They are also listed by CITES (see page 28), which controls trade in wild animals.

EXTREME ANIMALS

Mountain lions of North America can't roar like other big cats. Instead they have a distinctive high-pitched scream.

2.5 m

SAVING WILDLIFE

Snow leopard

There are fewer than 7,000 snow leopards left in the mountain regions of southern and central Asia. The Snow Leopard Trust has been working to save this endangered cat since the 1980s. It finds ways of protecting the leopards and their habitat, with the help of local communities. Although recovery is slow, the work of this and other organisations may one day see snow leopards off the danger list.

▼ *Snow leopards have thick fur to keep them warm, and large paws to help them walk on soft snow.*

Wild Dogs

Wolves, foxes and other wild members of the dog family stalk the grassy lower slopes of mountain ranges around the world. They usually feed on smaller creatures, but will sometimes attack farm animals.

WHAT DO YOU THINK?

Some wild dogs, including Himalayan wolves, are killed by farmers because they attack **livestock**. How can people be encouraged to save wildlife, even if it poses a threat to their livelihoods?

◀ *Himalayan wolves look similar to Tibetan wolves, a type of grey wolf. They have an orange-brown coat with patches of black and white.*

Himalayan wolves

Himalayan wolves survive in small areas of India and Nepal, high in the mountains. They may well represent the last surviving members of an ancient species of wolf. Their future remains uncertain and further research is necessary. Some wild wolves have been captured and are being bred in zoos in India, but they are not a protected species in all the countries in their range.

◀ *Tibetan sand foxes live high on the Tibetan* **Plateau***. They are not endangered, but are often killed by dogs.*

Singing dogs

Singing dogs of New Guinea once ranged across the whole of this island in the Pacific Ocean. Now, fewer than 200 of them live in the highland areas. The New Guinea Singing Dog Conservation Society campaigns for more research into these little-known wild dogs. It also encourages captive breeding, so that if the dogs die out in the wild the species will not become extinct.

▲ New Guinea singing dogs are so-called because their howl sounds like a song.

SAVING WILDLIFE

Ethiopian wolf

Ethiopian wolves are divided into seven small groups scattered throughout the mountains of Ethiopia, in North Africa. The Ethiopian Wolf Conservation Programme protects the remaining wolves, which number only around 500. Working with local communities is an important part of their conservation plan, to stop people killing the wolves.

▼ These Ethiopian wolves are in the Bale Mountains National Park in Ethiopia. Even here, the wolves have died from diseases such as **rabies**.

1 m

Hoofed Animals

Hardy and agile, hoofed animals such as sheep, goats and antelope can be found on mountain slopes even in some of the world's harshest and most remote regions.

Chiru

The Tibetan Plateau is a huge area of high ground that includes most of Tibet and parts of China and India. Within this harsh, rocky landscape the endangered antelope called the chiru survives. Severely hunted for its fine wool, in the past 100 years numbers of chiru have dropped from over a million to just 100,000. The Wildlife Conservation Society and the United States Fish and Wildlife Service have helped set up protected areas, and the antelope is now protected by law.

▲ *A male chiru watches over his herd of females in a nature reserve in Tibet.*

EXTREME ANIMALS

Himalayan yaks can live at higher altitudes than any other large **mammal**, up to 6,000 m.

2 m

Markhor

With no more than 2,500 markhor left in the mountains of Central Asia – through habitat loss and hunting for their unusual horns – these large goats are considered endangered. In India, some of them live in wildlife **sanctuaries**, but elsewhere they do not have this protection. In 1998, the Pakistan wildlife department joined with a team from the University of Montana, USA. They began working with local communities to stop markhor hunting.

▶ *Markhor are the largest species of goat in the world, known for their large, corkscrew horns.*

SAVING WILDLIFE

Vicuna

For centuries, wild vicunas of the Andes were hunted for their fur. By the early 1960s, only 10,000 remained in the wild. In 1964, they were made a protected species. At the same time, WWF, the Nature Conservancy and other conservation organisations established a nature reserve for the vicuna. These steps were successful – there are now 100,000 vicuna, and numbers are still rising. They are now ranked by the IUCN as of least concern.

Small Mammals

Hunting – for fur, food or to sell as pets – is one of the biggest dangers for small mountain creatures. This, together with habitat loss as forests are cleared and land is settled by people, has put many animals on the danger list.

Red pandas

People once thought red pandas were related to giant pandas. Although they eat bamboo like the bears, in fact they are more closely related to weasels. These mammals live in Himalayan mountain forests, but nearly half of them have died out in the past 50 years because of habitat loss and hunting. The 10,000 that are left are legally protected, but they are still taken by poachers and numbers are still dropping.

▲ *Red pandas are sometimes called firefoxes because of their colouring.*

Hares in the Himalayas

Hispid hares – nicknamed 'bristly rabbits' – were once found right across the foothills of the Himalayas. Now they are one of only two types of hare on the IUCN's list of endangered animals. Not much is known about them, and this makes planning conservation efforts difficult. Experts at WWF are finding out more about these rare hares, and the Conservation Leadership Programme (CLP) is also planning research that may save them.

▼ *Long-beaked echidnas are nocturnal animals, coming out at night to search for worms for food.*

19

Reptiles

**In the mountains live cold-blooded creatures –
from tiny lizards to large mugger crocodiles in the
marshy waters of the lower slopes. Snakes and
tortoises also live in some mountain zones.**

Snakes on the slopes

Snakes and other **reptiles** rely on the trees in mountain forests
and the rocks on the slopes for shelter. This means that they can
be badly affected when areas are cleared by **logging** or mining.
Conservation efforts are mainly focused on preserving or restoring
the habitat that has been damaged or lost by these activities.

▲ *Snakes, such as this Arizona
mountain kingsnake in the USA, live
beneath rocks on the mountain slopes.*

EXTREME ANIMALS

Rare Tibetan spring snakes all live around two hot springs in the Tibetan mountains. They may be the highest-altitude snakes in the world.

Lizards on the rocks

Like snakes, lizards often live beneath rocks, and spend daylight hours warming themselves in the sunshine. All sorts of lizards can be found in mountain environments, but as their habitat changes some are dying out. The Aran rock lizard of the Pyrénees, for example, has come under threat because of livestock grazing in its habitat, and because this is a popular place for ski resorts. The Aran lizard has now been included in an international agreement for conservation in the Pyrénees. It is hoped that saving the habitat may stop the lizards dying out.

▼ *The critically endangered Aran rock lizard was only discovered in 1993, in the Pyrénees mountains between France and Spain.*

Amphibians

The damp mountain habitat, which often has rivers and streams, is ideal for animals such as frogs, toads, salamanders and newts. These creatures live on land, but most need water in which to lay their eggs.

◀ *Baw baw frogs do not have webbed toes like many other frogs. Their skin is usually covered with tiny warts.*

Endangered Australian frogs

Several frogs of the high plateaus of southern Australia are endangered. One of the species most at risk is the baw baw frog, which is critically endangered. In the past 25 years, their numbers have dropped from around 10,000 to just 250. No one is sure why this has happened, but it may be because they are preyed on by feral animals. They are now protected by law, and the local government has put a recovery plan into action.

▼ *Yellow-legged frogs have adapted to live in icy mountain streams and other places too cold for many species.*

SAVING WILDLIFE

Yellow-legged frogs

Mountain yellow-legged frogs, of the Sierra Nevada mountains in the USA, are endangered. Experts believe that **pesticides** used on nearby farms might be carried on the wind and end up poisoning the frogs. Trout have also been introduced to the mountain rivers, and these fish often eat the tadpoles before they can grow into frogs. Some frogs are now being bred in captivity so they can be **reintroduced** into the wild.

Mountain salamanders

Like other **amphibians**, salamanders need to live close to a water source. They must keep their skin moist, and they lay their eggs in or near water. Endangered mountain salamanders include the cheat salamander in the USA and the Gorgan salamander in Iran. One of the most threatened is the Paghman salamander, found only in a very small area of Afghanistan. Although there are fewer than 2,000 left, wars and unrest in the country make it difficult for organisations to work on saving wildlife there.

▲ A cheat mountain salamander watches over its eggs in West Virginia, in the USA.

EXTREME ANIMALS

Alpine salamanders of the central and eastern Alps can have the longest **gestation** period of any animal – sometimes up to three years.

14 cm

Minibeasts

As a food source for small animals, insects and other minibeasts are a key part of the mountain environment. They help keep the habitat healthy by processes such as turning over the soil and pollinating **the flowers.**

▲ *Wekiu bugs have a special chemical in their blood that stops them freezing in their high, cold home.*

Wekiu bugs

The wekiu bug is an unusual insect. It lives around the **summit** of the volcano Mauna Kea, in Hawaii, where it feeds on other insects that are blown to high altitudes by the wind. Because it is so isolated this high up, experts are concerned about its future survival. Groups are monitoring populations and campaigning to make this bug a protected species.

SAVING WILDLIFE

Magazine Mountain middle-toothed snail

Native to the US state of Arkansas – and found only high up on Magazine Mountain – the middle-toothed snail is critically endangered. In an effort to save it from extinction, parts of the mountain have been made an Area of Special Interest, which means that people cannot build houses or roads there. Conservation groups are still campaigning for more protection, though, including research and control over the taking of the snails by collectors.

Few spiders are found at high altitudes, but Himalayan jumping spiders live extremely high up (up to 6,700 m).

2 cm

WHAT DO YOU THINK?

Conservation efforts often focus on larger creatures and ignore small but important insects and other minibeasts. How can we raise awareness of the importance of smaller creatures to Earth's habitats?

Alpine butterflies

Some alpine butterflies are thought to be under threat because of changes to their environment. Many butterflies need meadows to survive, because of the sunshine that reaches these areas and the flowers that grow there. Mountain forests are expanding, reducing the meadows and cutting off groups of butterflies from each other.

▶ *Apollo butterflies are nicknamed 'big eyes' because of the red eye marks on their wings.*

Birds

From low foothills and open alpine meadows, to craggy mountainous peaks, mountain environments are inhabited by all different species of birds.

SAVING WILDLIFE

Junin flightless grebe

The Junin flightless grebe is found only around Lake Junin in the highlands of Peru, South America. There are around 50–250 birds left, and it is critically endangered. Pollution from mining has affected the water in the lake. Although it was made a national reserve in the 1970s and a Ramsar site in 1997, conditions still worsened. In 2002, local groups pressured the Peruvian government into ordering a clean-up operation to save the birds.

▲ *The Junin grebe is one of the rarest birds in the world.*

Mountain finches

Cochabamba mountain finches are only found in mountain woodlands in Bolivia, South America. Although no one knows exactly how many survive there, it is thought to be fewer than 3,000. The American Bird Conservancy is working to protect and restore the finch's woodland habitat. It also carries out research on the birds and monitors populations where possible, which may help with further conservation efforts.

American owls

Saw-whet owls live in all North American mountain ranges, but their numbers are declining in several areas. This is mainly because logging has resulted in the loss of their forest homes. The Nature Conservancy is operating a programme in the southern Appalachian mountains to protect the habitat of the northern saw-whet owl and other creatures that live there.

▶ *Northern saw-whet owls use their brown feathers as camouflage in the trees during the day, and come out to hunt at night.*

Grouse of the Caucasus

The Caucasian grouse lives in the Caucasus mountains of Turkey. It is listed as near threatened by the IUCN. Activities such as mining, logging and building are widespread in many European mountain regions. Birdlife International has launched a campaign to address this issue. It hopes to raise awareness, and save not only mountain birds, but all the other creatures that make their homes in mountain regions.

What Can We Do?

The different mountain zones are home to many rare and diverse animals and plants, so it is important to make sure this unique environment is preserved to stop them dying out. All around the world, local, national and international organisations work hard to repair the damage already caused and to protect the wildlife that survives, but there are ways that everyone can help.

Find out more...

WWF *(www.wwf.org.uk)*
This is the UK site of the largest international animal conservation organisation. On this site you can follow links to information on all sorts of endangered animals and find out what WWF is doing to save mountain creatures.

EDGE of Existence *(www.edgeofexistence.org)*
EDGE of Existence is a special global conservation programme that focuses on saving what it calls evolutionarily distinct and globally endangered (EDGE) species – unusual animals and plants that are under threat.

International Union for Conservation of Nature *(www.iucn.org)*
The IUCN produces the Red List, which lists all the world's known endangered species and classifies them by how threatened they are, from least concern to extinct. You can see the whole list of endangered animals on the website, as well as discover what the IUCN does to address environmental issues all over the world.

Convention on International Trade in Endangered Species *(www.cites.org)*
CITES is an international agreement between governments that aims to ensure trade in wild animal species does not threaten their survival. It lists animals that are considered to be under threat from international trading and makes laws accordingly.

US Fish and Wildlife Service *(www.fws.gov)*
This government organisation was set up to manage and preserve wildlife in the USA. It helps manage wildlife reserves, including those in mountain regions, and makes sure laws that protect endangered animals are properly enforced.

Do more...

Sign a petition

Petitions are documents asking governments or organisations to take action on something people are concerned about. Some of the organisations opposite have online petitions that you can sign to show your support for their campaigns.

Go to the zoo

Find out if your local zoo is involved in any captive-breeding programmes and go along to find out more. Just visiting the zoo helps support these programmes.

Adopt an animal

For a small contribution to some conservation organisations you get to 'adopt' a mountain animal. They will send you information about your adopted animal, and keep you up to date on all the conservation efforts in the area in which it lives.

Spread the word

Find out as much as you can about the threats to mountain animals and what people are doing to save them, then tell your friends and family. The more support conservation organisations have, the more they can do!

Read more...

This is My Planet
by Jan Thornhill
(Franklin Watts, 2012)

Conservation Areas (Maps of the Environmental World)
by Jack and Meg Gillett
(Wayland, 2014)

Very Wonderful, Very Rare – Saving the Most Endangered Wildlife on Earth
by Baillie and Butcher
(Franklin Watts, 2013)

Every effort has been made by the publisher to ensure that these websites contain no inappropriate or offensive material. However, because of the nature of the Internet, it is impossible to guarantee that the content of these sites will not be altered. We strongly advise that Internet access is supervised by a responsible adult.

Mountain Animals Quiz

Take this quiz to see how much you can remember about mountain animals. Look back through the book if you need to. You can find the answers on page 32.

1. What is the longest mountain range in the world?

2. How does mining harm mountain habitats?

3. Why are bears of the Himalayan foothills endangered?

4. What is another name for the Andean bear?

5. How many giant pandas are there left?

6. Which critically endangered monkey has been named as a focal species by EDGE?

7. What three activities have endangered mountain gorillas?

8. What conservation efforts are helping endangered Arabian leopards?

9. Which organisation controls trade in wild animals such as Andean mountain cats?

10. Why do farmers in the Himalayas kill wolves?

11. How many groups of Ethiopian wolves are there left?

12. In which country are markhor protected in wildlife sanctuaries?

13. What IUCN ranking does the vicuna now have?

14. What do red pandas eat?

15. How many types of hare are listed as endangered by the IUCN?

16. Which animal preys on the Blue Mountain water skink?

17. In which mountain range does the endangered Aran rock lizard live?

18. Why are there no conservation efforts to save the Paghman mountain salamander?

19. Which unusual bug lives on the volcano Mauna Kea in Hawaii?

20. Which organisation is working to save the Cochabamba mountain finch of Bolivia?

Glossary

adapted changed in order to survive in new conditions.

alpine relating to high mountains.

altitude the height of something above the Earth's surface or above sea-level.

amphibians cold-blooded animals that spend some of their time on land and some in water.

captive breeding when endangered animals are specially bred in zoos or wildlife reserves so that they can then be released back into the wild.

civil war war between two groups in the same country.

commercial something that is done to make money.

conservation efforts to preserve or manage habitats when they are under threat, damaged or destroyed.

conservationists people who work to protect the natural environment.

continents the Earth's seven great landmasses – Africa, Antarctica, Asia, Australia, Europe, North America and South America.

deforestation the cutting down of large areas of forest.

endangered at risk of becoming extinct.

extinct when an entire species of animal dies out, so that there are none left on Earth.

felines animals that belong to the cat family.

feral animals that have gone back to being wild after being domesticated.

foothills hills at the base of a mountain.

fragmentation the breaking up of areas of forest by cutting down the trees between them.

gestation the period in which a baby grows inside its mother, before being born or hatching.

glaciers slow-moving rivers of ice.

global warming the rise in average temperatures around the world as a result of human activity.

habitat the place where an animal lives.

hibernation sleeping or not moving much in winter.

livestock animals kept by people for meat or milk.

logging cutting down trees to sell the wood for building or other uses.

mammal a warm-blooded animal that usually gives birth to live young.

minerals substances that occur naturally in the earth that people can use to make many different products.

native an animal that occurs naturally in a particular country or region.

pesticides chemicals often used by farmers to kill insects and other pests on their crops.

plateau an area of high land that is usually flat on top.

poaching hunting an animal when it is against the law to do so.

pollinating transferring pollen from one flower plant to another, so that it can make seeds and grow into a new plant.

protected species animals that are protected by law from hunting, trading or other human activities.

rabies a disease in animals that affects the nervous system and can be spread by biting.

reintroduced when animals that have been bred in captivity are let into the wild in areas where they once naturally occurred.

reptiles cold-blooded animals that lay eggs and usually have scales or plates on their skin.

reserves protected areas where animals can roam free and where the environment is carefully maintained for their benefit.

resources things that people can use for their own benefit, such as oil, coal and minerals.

sanctuaries special places where animals are protected or cared for if they are ill or injured.

species a type of animal or plant.

summit the very top of a mountain – its highest point.

Index

Numbers in **bold** indicate pictures

Quiz answers

1. Andes; 2. It clears the land and pollutes the soil; 3. Because of deforestation and hunting so that their body parts can be used in traditional medicine; 4. Spectacled bear; 5. About 1,600; 6. Yellow-tailed woolly monkey; 7. Forest clearance, poaching and civil war; 8. Establishing nature reserves, legal protection and captive breeding; 9. CITES; 10. Because they attack livestock; 11. Seven; 12. India; 13. Least concern; 14. Bamboo; 15. Two; 16. Cats; 17. Pyrénées; 18. War and unrest in Afghanistan, where they live; 19. Wekiu bug; 20. American Bird Conservancy.